Inspired by and learning from many great authors, speakers, and teachers, Patricia May has created this book compiling the thoughts, wisdom, concepts and practices and breaking them down in an easy understandable way kids can relate to. Using these different exercises and methods, Patricia has made a fun and creative way for kids to participate in daily practices to help give them the tools they need to make each day a more pleasant and peaceful experience. Everyday is gift. Each child has the opportunity to make it their best day imaginable.

Patricia May gives thanks to all those who have encouraged and motivated her to write these children's books in hopes to inspire kids to use these tools to create each day full of harmony and bliss.

Thank you:

Wayne Dyer - RIP - Created a better world through teachings of the law of attraction.

Abraham Hicks - Creating a life in a joyful happy way through choice of thoughts.

davidji - Making the world a better place through his teachings of meditation.

Anita Moorjani - Spreads words of hope and love, and teaches to never give up.

Rev. Pattie Weber - Teacher of love and light giving her all to keep us aligned.

Rev. Joe Hooper - Instills wisdom, love and acceptance to all around him.

James Van Praagh - Connecting us to the world beyond with enthusiasm and hope.

My family - Who inspires me daily just by being who they are.

HAPPY HAPPY

What is Happy?

Ask **anyone** that question and receive many different answers. What **happy** is to one person may not be the same for another. The **important** thing is to define what happy is to **you**.

We all know one thing about happy. When you **feel** it, you feel really good and joyful. Our hearts are **blissful**, our bodies are content, we smile and laugh. When you are **happy**, it not only affects you, but showers it's splendid radiance upon those around you.

Let's take a **journey** through this book and see just what you can do to be the happiest **joyful** person you can be.

Within the pages of this book you will find fun and simple daily exercises and practices to help create your physical, emotional and spiritual balance. When these three things work together in harmony, you feel more spiritually connected, physically stronger and emotionally happier. Practice one, two or as many of these every day to help provide the tools you need to be the happiest you, you can be!

Think Happy Thoughts

Say each affirmation out loud

I am **loved**   I listen to my **heart**   I am **safe**   I am **brave**

My dreams are coming **true**   What ever I do, I give my **best**

I can do **it**   I am just where I need to **be**   I am **important**

My heart is guiding me in the right **direction**   I love who I **am**

I think **positive**   I am grateful and **thankful**   I do **good** things

I have **courage**   I think happy **thoughts**   I respect **myself**

I am in charge of my **life**   I am thoughtful and **kind**

My friends are good and I am good to my **friends**

All Is Well

Make today a day worth while
By speaking words that make you smile
You know exactly how they feel
When you believe your words are real

HAPPY HAPPY HAPPY HAPPY HAPPY HAPPY HAPPY HAPPY

Be mindful of your thoughts for your thoughts become words

Be mindful of your words for your words become your actions

Be mindful of your actions for your actions show who you are

Be mindful of who you are for this is how you create your future.

3 Questions

* Each day as everyone gathers around the dinner table, ask these 3 questions, starting with one person and continuing around the table.

1. What is the best part about your day?

2. What is the one thing you love most about yourself today?

3. What one thing would you change about your day?

This is a fun and interactive way to express your thoughts and connect with others around you.

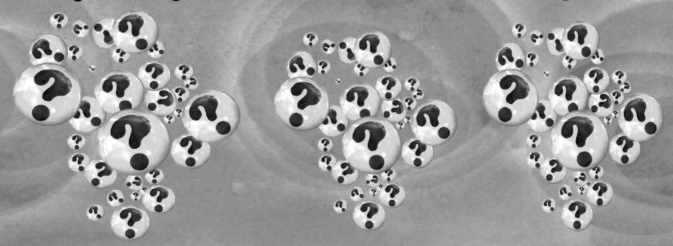

When **thinking** of your day and all that you have done,

happy

grateful

FUn

It's **important** you remember
to be **grateful** and have **fun.**

Time for Yoga

(Practice one pose daily)

The Many Benefits Yoga Offers

1. Helps develop body awareness

2. Teaches the use of your body in a healthy way

3. Manages stress through breathing, awareness, meditation and healthy movement

4. Builds concentration and focus

5. Increases confidence and positive self-image

6. Feel the connection with the mind, body and spirit

Create your happy
when you say,
I'll do my yoga
everyday.

Before school or after play,

It makes me strong
in every way.

Namaste

Mirror Play
(The Love Yourself Exercise)

Why? Because mirror play is a **loving gift**, you give **yourself**.

Mirror play is a process that takes the words you say and **reflects** them back to you. It doesn't get any more **real** than this. It makes you very **aware** of how your **thoughts** make you **feel**. If these **words** you say now are not the ones that make you feel **good**, try and use some **new** words and see if they make you feel any **better**. **Look** into the mirror as you **say** five things expressing how you **feel** about yourself at this moment. Once you finish, repeat the process only this time finish each sentence using the words below.

I am **happy** because I, _____

I **love** myself because, _____

I have great **ideas** and one of them is, _____

I am **perfect** the way I am, and my best quality is _____

I can do **anything** I put my mind to and today I will_____

When you look into the mirror what will your **heart** reveal?
The **words** you say **reflect** your mood and how you really feel.

When **showing** bliss
and being kind
your joyful
heart will **show**,
Exactly who you
really are
and happiness
will **flow**.

Inspire Imagine Create
Your Happy Journal

What do you love? What do you love to do?

Putting together a weekly journal can help clarify the thoughts in your mind when asking yourself these questions. Journaling can help inspire you to explore new directions, new activities, new interest you didn't even realize you might want to explore. Why not give it a try and see what shows up at the end of each week through your journal.

Cut out pictures from a magazine or book on these subjects.

1. Career. Cut out jobs or careers that sound interesting to you.

2. Colors. Cut out the colors your eyes are drawn to most.

3. Interest. Cut out the things that look interesting to you.

4. Activities. Cut out activities that look like they might be fun and exciting.

5. Places. Cut out places you would like to go.

Tape or glue your cut outs on construction paper. Do this everyday for 7 days. At the end of 7 days, lay out all pages you have put together. Do you see similarities in the themes, topics or ideas? This exercise may be showing you something that may have been hidden in your subconscious mind and now has been brought forth for you to explore. It's time to begin a new adventure.

Follow your heart and see what sparks your imagination.

When you imagine what you want
And what you want to do,
Your ideas flow from head to toe
Creating dreams for you.

A Seashell Meditation

Find a space sit comfortably and hold your little shell,

Up to your ear now close your eyes and know that all is well.

Take a breath quite slowly as you feel the peace within,

Now blow out slow, relax your mind and now we will begin.

This simple meditation is to quiet down the mind,

While focusing on happiness our joy and being kind.

Attention to our thoughts and words will help to motivate,

The actions you will need to take in order to create.

As you move throughout your life deciding what you'll do,

Your heart will guide in every way and help your dreams come true.

It's your decision as you choose the life that you desire,

Thinking of the things you love that lights your heart on fire.

Following your inner voice will always lead the way,

To happiness and feeling good and joyful every day.

Inspiration sparks your thoughts your ideas come alive,

This is when your energy starts pushing you to thrive.

You know that you have found your bliss and happiness inside,

When all you feel is peace and love you carry it with pride.

Put down your shells open your eyes and take a breath in deeply,

Blow out slow, stretch out your arms relax your mind completely.

Remember you can do this meditation anywhere,

Your happiness and joyful heart will always be right there.

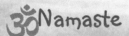 Namaste

A Daily Mindful Exercise~~~Inspires Imagination & Creativity

Reduce stress & anxiety

Increase self confidence and awareness

Improve heart health

Boost mood and immunity

Promote better sleep habits

Decrease aggression

Create calmness

Develops clarity

Encourages stabilty

A meditation everyday
Improves your life in many ways
So close your eyes relax your mind
Serenity is what you'll find.

Find Happiness in Nature

The outdoors is a fabulous place to stimulate all your senses, energize the mind, get in touch with your emotions and perfect for physical development. Interacting with nature allows learning by doing and helps clear the mind in order to explore new ideas. Find some time each day to mingle with nature. Here are just a few things for you to do for fun while being out amongst the beauty in our world.

Cloud Gazing. Look at the shapes and imagine what they look like.

Listen to birds. How many can you hear?

Make a fort. Bring out some towels and blankets. Make your perfect hide a way.

Pick flowers. Put together a beautiful arrangement using all kinds of plants and flowers.

Climb up trees. Take a book and read while sitting up on your favorite tree branch.

Collect rocks. Find some smooth surfaced rocks and write inspiring words on them with your colored sharpies. Then put them all around the house and out in the yards.

Go on a bike ride. Grab your friends and take a ride on a scenic trail.

Create a garden. Plant some flower, vegetable or fruit seeds and watch your garden grow.

Gather leaves. Find some beautiful leaves and use them in a fun craft project.

Seashell. Search for seashells along the seashore. Put them in a jar and set them on your dresser.

Hike. Take a hike and explore all the beauty around you. Notice the variety nature offers.

Sit by the river. Listen to the trickling sounds of the river and watch it's flowing pathways.

Attitude of Gratitude
The Quality of Being Thankful

Showing acts of kindness, appreciation and being thankful is a very rewarding and motivating process. Gratitude is a selfless act. It shows others unconditionally that they are appreciated.

It's rewards are great when gratitude is used with positive emotions.

There are many ways to show gratitude. This exercise is a wonderful example of what having an attitude of gratitude is all about.

1. Find a picture of someone close to you, someone you love, look up to, or admire.

2. Tape this picture onto a piece of construction paper.

3. Each day for 7 days, write one word on this paper around the picture you chose expressing why you are happy to have this person in your life.

4. After 7 days, give this person your completed project.

*You have just given and shown your gratitude to another, who will now know they are appreciated by you. This exchange creates benefits for you and for the one receiving. Now begin a new project and continue this exercise each week.

Outside is the place to be

Hike through hills climb up the trees

Collect seashells out by the sea

Enjoy fresh air and feel the breeze

Benefits of Gratitude

Improve Health
& Wellbeing

Create Positivity

Become More
Optimistic

Share Kindness

Boost Energy

Increase Self Esteem

Deeper Relationships

Grateful Behaviour

Enhance Self Worth

When showing others that you care
with honest attitude,
Your happiness is strengthened through
Your giving gratitude.

Do the Happy Dance

Why Dance?

Music and dancing can lift your spirits when you're feeling down, sad or lonely. Dancing to the music gives your body exercise while moving around and having fun. It boost your energy levels, improves body movement, heart health, lungs, muscle tone and your strength all while having fun and doing what comes naturally. It's a great way to release the chemicals in you're brain that raise your vitality and make you feel good. Put on your favorite song. Get moving around, dance like no one is watching. Perhaps make up a routine, new exercise moves, or sing karaoke. Keep going until your song ends.

Dance is a great way to release tension, anxiety, and nervousness.

Listen to your favorite song Get up and dance around
Flap your arms and move your legs By jumping up and down

It doesn't matter if you dance

While others are around

Just close your eyes, feel happiness

Keep moving to the sound.

Take a **breath** and feel your chest as it begins to rise,

Now exhale very slowly as it's time we close our eyes.

Breathe in deep and hold right there up to the count of three,

Let's blow out slow and just **relax,** sit still and let it be.

Imagine we have **spinning** wheels of energy and light,

That **line up** through our bodies as their colors shine so bright.

These little wheels of **energy** give health and wellness too,

And keep us **balanced** as we learn through practices we do.

Chakra is the name we give these **seven little wheels,**

And now we'll learn just what they **do** and see what they reveal.

The colors of our chakras match the **rainbow** in the sky,

Discover what each color means just how they **work** and **why.**

Red is first beginning at the bottom of our spine,

It's called the **root** it keeps us grounded stable and aligned.

Orange the sacral gives us thoughts of creativity,

Below the navel this is where we get our **energy.**

Keep Your

Keeping chakras
Restores
And helps to keep
And live

Chakras Happy

Yellow is our solar plexus right below the chest,
Self esteem and confidence is what it's known for best.
Green is for the healing it's location is the heart,
Tranquility and balance helps us never fall apart.
Blue is for communicating from your throat so clear,
And this is where your voice of light comes from for all to hear.
Indigo's imagination right between the brows,
Called the third eye this is where awareness will arouse.
Violet is your crown beyond and this is where you'll find,
Connection from your very best to all that is Divine.
Red, orange, yellow, green, blue, indigo and violet too,
Are all your chakra colors now you know just what they do.
Time again to take a breath and blow it out with ease,
Open your eyes it's time to give your hands a great big squeeze.
Keep flowing energy and light through all your spinning wheels,
By simply meditating and remembering how this feels.

flowing free
their energy
your body well
life happily.

Spend   Save   Share

You can not give what you do not have. In order to share, you must first give to yourself. Be kind and loving to yourself, then share this kindness and love with others.

Being charatable fills the heart. It is called being compassionate. It is these things that help to make the world a better place.

Here is a fun project. Get 3 mason jars and decorate them as you like. Tie bows, ribbon or rope around the tops. Then make 3 labels. Spend, Save and Share. Glue or tie the labels onto your jars. Begin filling your jars with money. Money you earn, find or perhaps are given. Once all 3 jars are full, it is time to spend, you earned it, save, by putting your savings into a bank account or bigger jar, and then decide who or where you would like to give your "share" money. Doing this act of giving, creates a ripple affect through more people than you can even imagine. Being kind to others, is being kind to yourself. Keep up the good work.

When **giving** from your heart with love
Compassion flows throughout,

The world **becomes** a better place
That's what it's all **about.**

Sparkle Your Way to Calmness
The Calming Jars

There are times when you might feel angery, frustrated, upset, sad, nervous or anxious. It's what you do in these times that matter. Before these emotions get out of control, there are ways to help find your way back to peace, tranquility and happiness. This works for all ages and it's fun!

What you will need to make your calming bottles.

1. Plastic Voss water bottle, plastic jar or any clear smooth plastic bottle.
2. 4 oz clear bottle of (elmers) glue.
3. Colored glitter
4. Warm water.
5. Marble, mini lego toy, or any small object.

Now, get your jar or empty Voss water bottle.

Squeeze the entire bottle of clear 4 oz glue into the plastic jar or water bottle.

2. Drop in marble, toy or small object.
3. Put in glitter about 1/4 cup.
4. And fill remainder with warm tap water.
5. Shake, shake, shake, until all it mixed up well.

*Foam will subside from top of bottle once settled.

It's always great when you feel happy, joy and bliss, but there are many more emotions we feel on a daily basis. There are ways to acheive better feelings through the thoughts you choose. Using the calming jar is one way to help bring releif when you feel depressed, anger, or sadness. When feeling hopeful and happy, the calming jar will help keep you in the present moment while experiencing hopeful and happy thoughts. Keep your jar in a special place. Once a day, or when you feel you need it, grab your jar and sit comfortably on a pillow, rug or chair. Shake until mixed. Set it down on a hard surface or table top. As you watch the glitter settling to the bottom, breathe in and out very slow, continuing this breathing while watching the glitter until all is settled.

Benefits of calming jars

1. Focus attention
2. Takes focus off negitive emotions
3. Gives moments to calm down
4. Allows chance to solve problems
5. Helps manage emotions.

Shake your jar and watch the sparkles floating gracefully
Inspire thoughts of joy while breathing slow and easily
Imagine your heart filled with love and positivity
Believe each day will bring you hope and perfect harmony.

Happy	Belief	Doubt	Hate	Fear
Joyful	Hopeful	Sadness	Rage	Depressed
Blissful	Positive	Dissapointment	Anger	Worthless

16 Seconds to Happiness

Performing this exercise each day, several times a day if you wish, brings a sense of instant calming, releases stress, and creates the space of being present in the moment. Yes, just 16 seconds, something you can do anywhere and anytime you wish. Give it a try and feel the sensation of peace flow within you. Then, go about doing what you do in a more relaxed and mellow way.

Close your eyes and slowly inhale as you count to 4.

Feeling relaxed and clearing your mind, hold there for a count of 4.

Slowly release all tension as you blow out counting to another 4.

Hold there for another count of 4, open your eyes and feel refreshed.

I Found My Happy!

I Found My Happy!

I Found My Happy!

I Found My Happy!

I Found My Happy!

When looking for your **happiness** It's certain you will find,

Exactly what you're looking for Is in your heart and mind.

Think your thoughts be **positive** Be grateful true and kind,

By **practicing** these daily tasks You'll never fall behind.

About the Author

Patricia May became an author in 2015 after attending a Hay House event in Denver Colorado. Inspired by a davidji seminar, Patricia wrote the first book, Seashell Meditations for Children, followed by Under the Sea, The A'B'C's of Meditation, The Unicorn Without a Horn, The Bear with Curly Hair and her latest, Find Your Happy. Writing books that inspire a kids imagination is her passion. Encouraging kids to find that spark within, is her goal.

Patricia is honored to have davidji, Hay House author, radio show host, meditation teacher and speaker write the testimonial for the Seashell Meditation books and Anita Moorjani, a Hay House author, speaker, and a New York Times best selling author endorse, Find Your Happy.

Patricia lives in the foothills of Sacramento California with her husband, poodles, and her kids and grandkids living not too far away.

www.booksthatinspireakidsimagination.com

Made in the USA
Middletown, DE
15 May 2021